The Raindrop Who Couldn't Fall

Written by:
Kirsti Call

Illustrated by:
Lisa M. Griffin

To My Five
Little Raindrops
KC

The Raindrop Who Couldn't Fall

Softcover (paper) ISBN: 978-1-946124-36-4
Hardcover (cloth) ISBN: 978-1-946124-35-7
Second Edition

Text Copyright © 2018 Kirstine Erekson Call

Published by
Mazo Publishers ~ P.O. Box 10474
Jacksonville, Florida 32247 USA
Tel: 1-815-301-3559

Website: www.mazopublishers.com
Email: mazopublishers@gmail.com

Library of Congress Cataloging-in-Publication Data
Call, Kirstine
"The Raindrop Who Couldn't Fall" / written by Kirstine Call, Illustrated by Lisa M. Griffin.

Summary: "The Raindrop Who Couldn't Fall" is a children's picture book for ages 3 to 7. It is based on the idea that changing your thought patterns can change the outcome of events in your life. The main character, Plink, is unable to fall from her cloud until she changes the way she thinks about falling and starts to believe in her abilities. The book is peppered with fun facts about the water cycle, cloud formation, and the science of rainbows (among other facts), making it appeal to the older readers in this age range. Includes supplementary material for parents and / or teachers, author / illustrator bios, and a glossary.
[1. Children's - Fiction 2. Education]

All Rights Reserved.
No part of this publication may be translated, reproduced, stored in a retrieval system, or transmitted in any form or by any means, electronic, mechanical, photocopying, recording or otherwise, without prior permission in writing from the publisher.

Plink was a little raindrop
who lived on a cloud over Watertown.

Most little drops liked jumping on clouds before bedtime.

Plink did too.

Most little drops loved icy desserts.

Plink did too.

And most little drops longed to be part of a beautiful

Rainbow.

Plink did too.

The
Water Cycle
shows how the water on earth travels in a circle from the land, up to the sky, and back down again to the land.

But Plink had a problem.
She could not fall.

All of her friends fell out of the sky easily, but Plink could not fall.

She tried jumping off her cloud.
Nothing happened.

She squeezed her eyes shut and tried diving.

Nothing happened.

She climbed on top of her cloud and tried spinning to the ground. Nothing happened.

Plink was afraid she would be stuck – on her cloud – spinning forever.

Clouds are made of tiny droplets of water or ice. The droplets are so small and light that they float in the air.

Her sister, her friends, her cousins, and her neighbors laughed and played and fell any time they wanted.

Plink watched *glumly*. She felt tears *prickling* the corners of her eyes, but then she thought of Grandmother.

Grandmother always knew what to do.

States of Matter

Water comes in three different forms.

The solid form is ice.
The liquid form is water.
The gas form is steam.

Plink found Grandmother making ice crystals for raindrop training.

"Why are you so sad my little drop?"

"Grandmother,
What's the matter with me?
I try so hard but I cannot fall.
Ping can fall!
Plunk and Patter can fall, too!
But I can't, no matter what I do!"

Grandmother's warm arms *enveloped* her. "Plink, some raindrops take longer to learn the art of falling off a cloud.

Keep working. It will happen."

So Plink kept practicing.

She imagined herself floating down to give a flower a drink.

She imagined landing on the head of a playful kitten.

Evaporation is when the *molecules* that make up a liquid heat up enough to escape in the form of a gas.

Condensation is when *water vapor* in the air cools and sticks together to form drops of water that become rain.

Every day she practiced,

and every day she watched helplessly as everyone in her town worked together to create splashes of light and color and

glorious rain.

Plink was stuck on her cloud **during raindrop training,** as all the other little raindrops practiced falling in perfectly *synchronized* circles.

Plink strained forward, *willing herself to fall.* Instead, she spun wildly, crashing into some classmates and breaking their circle.

"Hey, watch where you're going!" Patter yelled. "You'll never learn to fall! You're too *clumsy*!" agreed Ping.

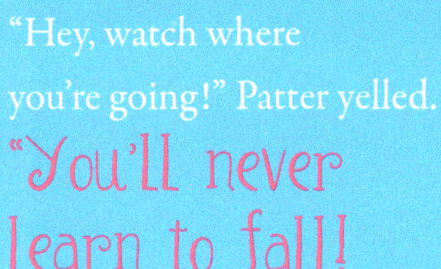

Rainfall

Rain falls when too many raindrops squeeze together within a cloud, making the tiny drops bump together to form bigger, heavier drops. These larger drops are too heavy to float, so they fall.

Plink hung her head.

They were right.
She was never going to learn.

She sniffled, then cried, watching tears
drift slowly to the ground.
Drip... drip... drip... until PLOP!

Plink suddenly *realized* something that gave
her hope!
Perhaps Grandmother's *advice*
was right, after all.
Plink's heart pounded
as a whole new attitude *engulfed* her.

She took a deep breath

to *steady* herself, smiling through her tears.

Plink was smiling because she realized

that if her tears could fall, then maybe

she could fall too!

Plink felt stronger.

She felt more *confident*.

And she felt grateful.

She imagined herself

floating down, gently landing in

the meadow below.

That's when it happened.

Plink grabbed Grandmother's hand. Grandmother always knew she could do it. And now, hand in hand with Grandmother, **Plink knew she could** do it, too.

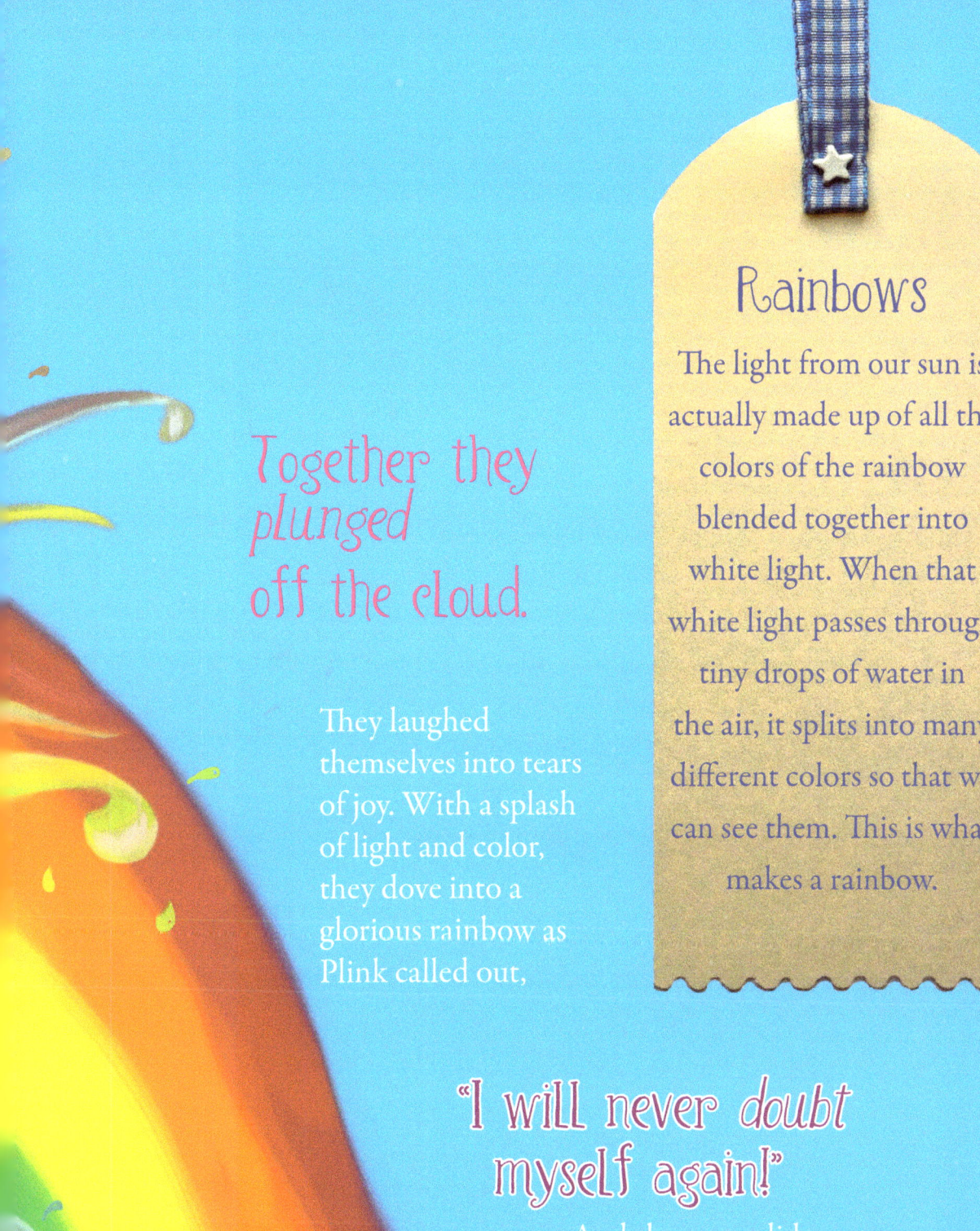

Together they plunged off the cloud.

They laughed themselves into tears of joy. With a splash of light and color, they dove into a glorious rainbow as Plink called out,

Rainbows

The light from our sun is actually made up of all the colors of the rainbow blended together into white light. When that white light passes through tiny drops of water in the air, it splits into many different colors so that we can see them. This is what makes a rainbow.

"I will never *doubt* myself again!"

And she never did.

GLOSSARY

Advice:	Words of guidance
Clumsy:	Ungraceful in movement
Condensation:	To make smaller by squeezing parts closer together
Confident:	Believing in yourself
Doubt:	Uncertainty
Engulfed:	To swallow up or surround
Enveloped:	Wrapped up or surrounded
Evaporation:	Changing from liquid to gas
Glumly:	Full of gloom or sadness
Matter:	Anything that takes up space
Molecule:	The very smallest piece of something
Plunged:	To throw yourself suddenly
Prickling:	Tingling
Realized:	Understood
Steady:	Calm and still
Synchronized:	Moving all at the same time, or together
Water Vapor:	Water in its gas form
Willing:	Making something happen by wanting it badly

Projects

WATER CYCLE GAME: SUN, CLOUD, RAIN
(based on Rock, Paper, Scissors)
Number of kids: 2 or more

Directions:
1. Find a partner.
2. Facing each other, tap your fists in your open palms two times.
3. The 3rd time, use your hand to form one of three items: Sun, Cloud, or Rain.
4. Repeat and have fun!
- Sun conquers Rain. (evaporation) For Sun, spread your fingers pointing upward.
- Cloud conquers Sun. (condensation) For Cloud, keep your hand in a fist.
- Rain conquers Cloud. (precipitation) For Rain, spread fingers pointing downward.

If playing with more than 2 people, the winner plays another person who has won until the last 2 people compete to become champion!

MERINGUE CLOUDS
Yields: 16 to 18 cookies
- 2 large egg whites
- 1/8 teaspoon cream of tartar
- 1/2 cup granulated sugar
- 1/4 tsp vanilla

Directions:
1. Preheat oven to 200 degrees. ONLY DO THIS WITH YOUR PARENTS' PERMISSION!
2. Beat egg whites on medium speed until they develop foamy bubbles.
3. Add cream of tartar and whisk on medium-high speed until whites form peaks.
4. Add sugar to egg whites in a slow stream and beat until soft peaks become glossy and stiff. Beat in vanilla.
5. Use a teaspoon to drop meringue cookies onto a parchment-lined baking sheet.
6. Bake for 1 hour and 40 minutes, or until cookies are crisp on the outside, but not brown. Remove from oven and cool on a rack. Store in airtight container for up to 4 days.

HOW TO MAKE A RAINBOW:
Go outside and face your shadow. Use a hose with a nozzle and spray water at a 40 degree angle to the right of your shadow.

HOW TO MAKE RAINSTICKS
Rainsticks are musical instruments that people in Chile make to encourage more rainfall.

Materials needed:
- rice, dried lentils, unpopped popcorn or tiny pasta
- paper towel or toilet paper tube
- aluminum foil
- scissors
- duct tape
- markers or paint

1. Cap the end of your tube with tape.
2. Cut a piece of aluminum foil that is about one and half times the length of your tube and about 6 inches wide.
3. Crunch the aluminum foil into two long thin snake like shapes. Twist each snake into a coil.
4. Put both coils in the tube.
5. Fill the bottom 2" of the tube with rice (or substitute).
6. Cap the other end of your tube with tape.
7. Decorate the tube with markers or paint.
8. Slowly turn the tube end-over-end and listen to the sound of your own homemade rain!

Kirsti Call

lives near Watertown, MA with her husband and five children. She loves reading, writing, and singing. On sunny days you will find her on the tire swing in her backyard, and on rainy days you will find her dancing with her umbrella.

Lisa M. Griffin

is an illustrator specializing in stories for children. She spends most days in her cozy New Hampshire studio enjoying a cup of tea while sketching and working on picture books. When she isn't drawing and daydreaming, Lisa enjoys reading, yoga, photography, and time with her family.

Lisa holds a BFA in Visual Design & Illustration and is a member of SCBWI.

How the Art was made...

it all began with a pencil and some paper. Small sketches are made to show how the art will appear in the book and scanned into the computer. Color is added using digital painting techniques. Creating a children's books is a wonderful project but very time consuming - the art in this picture book took many, many months to complete!

Pencil sketch of the cover "The Raindrop Who Couldn't Fall"

www.ingramcontent.com/pod-product-compliance
Lightning Source LLC
Chambersburg PA
CBHW041433040426
42451CB00021B/3495